Dear Mrs. Francis,

Thank you so much for all of your help and support!

From,

Alessandra Fusco
and family

Words of
Compassion

Words of Compassion

COMPILED BY SAMANTHA GRAY
DESIGNED BY DAVID FORDHAM

CICO BOOKS

LONDON NEW YORK

Published in 2009 by CICO Books
An imprint of
Ryland Peters & Small
20–21 Jockey's Fields   519 Broadway, 5th Floor
London WC1R 4BW   New York, NY 10012

10 9 8 7 6 5 4 3 2 1

Design and illustrations © CICO Books 2009

A CIP catalog record for this book is available from the Library of Congress
and the British Library.

ISBN-13: 978 1 906525 48 4

Printed in China

Designer: David Fordham

Contents

Introduction

WE SHOW PEOPLE we care through our actions and with comforting physical gestures—a hug or a sympathetic smile—but mainly we communicate through words. At times of sadness or crisis, we have all experienced the difference a few kind words can make—all the more so when what is said demonstrates empathy with how we feel. It is comforting to know that others have felt just as we do, and found strength to face life's challenges with courage and acceptance.

To me, reading the words people have chosen to express compassion demonstrates the importance of a sense of connection to our fellow human beings and to higher goals than our own personal day-to-day concerns. In reaching out to others, we open our hearts and minds to feel as they feel, and to see the world as they see it. Compassion, as the Dalai Lama points out, sounds simple but actually takes thoughtfulness, energy, imagination, and generosity of spirit to achieve.

Working as a relationship therapist, I see people focusing their energy on keeping alive that precious sense of emotional connection to their partners. It takes courage to share one's true self with another person and to give loving acceptance to them in return. There is maturity in tolerating that person's differences, which may not match with expectations or ideals.

The society we live in has become increasingly narcissistic with many people going into every situation, including relationships, with a "what's in it for me?" attitude. But how much better would it be to think of others first? To embrace the challenge of really loving and standing by those we care about no matter what happens, thus demonstrating true compassion? As one man—part of a couple who faced terrible life crises, including cancer—said to me only yesterday: "We get things wrong for each other, we fall out with each other, but we truly love each other. I love her deeply. I love her with no hair after chemo. I know I still love her even when she's being snappy. I deeply love the unique person she is."

When love joins with compassion, humanity is at its best—something, I think, that has been recognized by all the authors of the quotes on the following pages. *Words of Compassion* brings together quotes from world-renowned celebrities and from anonymous authors and thinkers, from those blessed with material wealth and those whose wealth is of the spirit, and from those with a long life before them and those facing their own mortality. All provide reassurance and renew our strength of purpose to let compassion inform all that we do and say.

"ALWAYS BE A LITTLE KINDER THAN NECESSARY."

James M. Barrie (1860–1937)

"*It is my belief, for the world in general, that compassion is more important than 'religion.'*"

Tenzin Gyatso, the 14th Dalai Lama
(1935–)

Chapter One

THE POWER OF KINDNESS

" KINDNESS
is the
GREATEST WISDOM."

ANONYMOUS

" *Three* THINGS IN HUMAN LIFE ARE
IMPORTANT.
THE *First* IS TO BE KIND.
THE *Second* IS TO BE KIND.
AND THE *Third* IS TO BE KIND."

HENRY JAMES (1843–1916)

"I expect to pass through life but once.
If, therefore, there be any

KINDNESS

I can chow,

or any good thing I can do

to any fellow being,

let me do it now,

and not defer or neglect it,

as I shall not pass this way again."

WILLIAM PENN (1644–1718)

"THOSE WHO BRING *sunshine*
TO THE LIVES OF OTHERS
CANNOT KEEP
it
FROM THEMSELVES."

JAMES MATTHEW BARRIE (1860–1937)

"THERE IS NOTHING
STRONGER
IN THE WORLD THAN *tenderness.*"

HAN SUYIN (Chinese author, 1917–)

*"When I was young,
I admired clever people.
Now that I am old,
I admire kind people."*

ABRAHAM JOSHUA HESCHEL (1907–1972)

"IN SEPARATENESS

lies the world's GREAT misery,

IN COMPASSION
lies the world's true STRENGTH."

GAUTAMA BUDDHA
(563–483 BCE)

"*The little unremembered acts of*
KINDNESS AND LOVE
are the best parts of a person's life."

WILLIAM WORDSWORTH (1770–1850)

"*Next to love,*
SYMPATHY
is the divinest passion
of the HUMAN HEART."

EDMUND BURKE (1729–1797)

"It is logic that SOMEONE who is *privileged* should do SOMETHING for those who are not."

AUDREY HEPBURN (1929–1993)

"THE TRUE *measure of a man* IS HOW HE TREATS SOMEONE WHO CAN DO HIM *absolutely no good*."

DR SAMUEL JOHNSON (1709–1784)

"A KIND WORD IS LIKE A
Spring day."

RUSSIAN PROVERB

"*The kindest word
in all the world
is the unkind word,
unsaid.*"

ANONYMOUS

" *I would rather make mistakes in* kindness *and* compassion *than work miracles in unkindness and* hardness. "

BLESSED MOTHER TERESA OF CALCUTTA (1910–1997)

"WORDS have the POWER
to both DESTROY
and HEAL.

When WORDS are both
TRUE and KIND,
they can change
OUR WORLD."

GAUTAMA BUDDHA
(563–483 BCE)

"There are many beautiful people in the world, but she had that extra thing, which is really genuine warmth because she had a loving and compassionate heart."

BARBARA DALY ON PRINCESS DIANA

Chapter Two

A

LOVING

HEART

"I don't think *what you* **LOOK** like is important. I think it's *what you* **ARE** that's important. I think *what you* **are** really makes *what you* **look** like."

"Everybody wants
to be validated."

OPRAH WINFREY (1954–)

"It is IMPORTANT to accept
each other as we are, that is
the beginning of LOVE."

BLESSED MOTHER TERESA OF CALCUTTA (1910–1997)

" TO SEE, IT IS NOT ENOUGH TO OPEN THE EYES. ONE MUST FIRST ALSO OPEN ONE'S HEART. "

GASTON REBUFFAT (French mountaineer, 1921–1985)

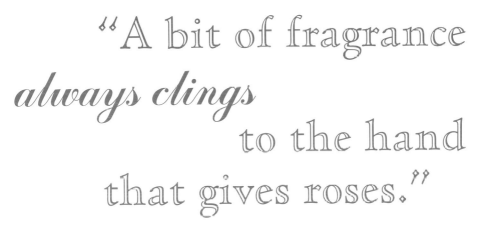

"A bit of fragrance *always clings* to the hand that gives roses."

CHINESE PROVERB

"In the dew of LITTLE THINGS the heart finds its morning and is REFRESHED."

KAHLIL GIBRAN (1883–1931)

"I always prefer to believe the BEST of everybody; it saves so much trouble."

RUDYARD KIPLING (1865–1936)

"Don't wait for people to be friendly: show them how."

ANONYMOUS

"*The worst sin towards our fellow creatures is not to hate them, but to be indifferent to them:* THAT'S THE ESSENCE OF INHUMANITY."

GEORGE BERNARD SHAW (1856–1950),
from *The Devil's Disciple*

"THE *dew* OF COMPASSION IS A *tear*."

LORD BYRON (1788–1824)

"*Make* NO *judgments where you have* NO *compassion.*"

ANONYMOUS

"YOU ARE GOOD

WHEN YOU ARE ONE WITH YOURSELF."

KAHLIL GIBRAN (1883–1931)

"Whatever you do,
trample down abuses,
And love those who love you."

VOLTAIRE (1694–1778)

"When people are dying, they are much more o p e n and more VULNERABLE, and much more REAL than other people."

DIANA, PRINCESS OF WALES (1961–1997)

"THE BIGGEST DISEASE THIS WORLD SUFFERS FROM IS THE DISEASE OF PEOPLE FEELING UNLOVED, *and I know that I can give love.*"

DIANA, PRINCESS OF WALES (1961–1997)

" *Compassion and love are precious things in life. They are not complicated. They are simple but difficult to practice.* "

TENZIN GYATSO, THE 14TH DALAI LAMA (1935–)

"YOU WILL FIND AS YOU LOOK BACK UPON YOUR LIFE THAT THE MOMENTS WHEN YOU HAVE TRULY LIVED ARE THE MOMENTS WHEN YOU HAVE DONE THINGS IN THE SPIRIT OF LOVE."

HENRY DRUMMOND (1851–1897)

"Don't think about how many moments you have left; rather endeavour to live as much as possible in each moment."

AMBUJ SHARMA

" *While we are mourning*
the loss of our friend,
others are rejoicing
to meet him behind
the veil."

JOHN TAYLOR
(American politician, senator, and philosopher,
1753–1824)

Chapter Three

LOVE IS STRONGER THAN DEATH

"Yet **meet** we shall, and
p a r t, and **meet** again,
Where dead men **meet** on
lips of living men."

SAMUEL BUTLER (1835–1902)

*"Better by far you should forget
and smile
Than that you should remember
and be sad."*

CHRISTINA ROSSETTI (1830–1894)

" *Love* FLIES, R U N S,
and REJOICES: *it is free*
and nothing can hold it
back. "

THOMAS À KEMPIS (1380–1471)

"THOSE WHO LOVE
DEEPLY
NEVER GROW OLD;
THEY MAY DIE OF
OLD AGE,
BUT THEY DIE YOUNG."

SIR ARTHUR PINERO (English dramatist, 1855–1934)

"*I* have learned that some of the ***nicest*** people you'll ever meet are those who have suffered a traumatic event or loss. *I* ***admire*** them for their ***strength***, but most especially for their ***life gratitude*** —a gift often taken for granted by the average person in society."

SASHA AZEVEDO (Actress and model, 1978–)

"I hold it true, whate'er befall
I feel it, when I sorrow most;
'Tis better to have LOVED *and* LOST
Than never to have LOVED *at all."*

LORD ALFRED TENNYSON (1809–1892)

" TO LIVE IN THE HEARTS WE LEAVE BEHIND IS NOT TO DIE."

THOMAS CAMPBELL (Scottish poet, 1777–1844)

"I BELIEVE THAT TEARS
CAN HEAL,
THAT MEMORIES
CAN COMFORT,
THAT LOVE LIVES ON
FOREVER."

ANONYMOUS

"*Four* angels to my bed
Four angels round my head
One to watch, and *one* to pray
And *two* to bear my soul away."

Thomas Ady (17th century)

"*He spake well who said*
THAT GRAVES
are the
FOOTPRINTS OF ANGELS."

Henry Wadsworth Longfellow (1807–1882)

"A good character is the best tombstone.

Those who loved you
and were helped by you
will remember you
when forget-me-nots
have withered.
Carve your name
on hearts,
not on marble."

CHARLES H. SPURGEON (British Baptist preacher, 1834–1892)

"LOVE IS IMMORTALITY."

EMILY DICKINSON (1830–1886)

"*Death leaves
a heartache*
NO ONE *can heal
Love leaves a
memory*
NO ONE *can steal.*"

FROM A HEADSTONE IN IRELAND

"Perhaps,

they are not stars,

but rather openings in Heaven.

Where the *love* of our lost ones

pours down

through and shines

upon us

to let us know they are *happy*."

Eskimo legend

"WHEN YOU ARE sorrowful look again IN YOUR HEART, and you shall SEE THAT in truth you are weeping for THAT which has been YOUR DELIGHT."

KAHLIL GIBRAN (1883–1931)

"Doubt *thou the stars are fire;*
Doubt *that the sun doth move*
Doubt *Truth to be a liar:*
But never doubt *I love.*"

WILLIAM SHAKESPEARE (1564–1616), from *Hamlet*

"IF I EVER BECOME A SAINT,
I WILL SURELY BE ONE OF DARKNESS.
I WILL CONTINUALLY BE ABSENT
FROM HEAVEN
TO LIGHT THE LIGHT
OF THOSE IN DARKNESS ON EARTH."

BLESSED MOTHER TERESA OF CALCUTTA (1910–1997)

"I'm aware that people I have loved
and have died are in the spirit world
looking after me."

DIANA, PRINCESS OF WALES (1961–1997)

" *Farewell to thee! but not farewell*
*To all my fondest thoughts
of thee:
Within my heart they still
shall dwell;
And they shall cheer and
comfort me.*"

ANNE BRONTË (1820–1849)

Chapter Four

LAST WORDS

"DEATH
is only a larger kind of
GOING ABROAD."

Samuel Butler (1835–1902)

" LIFE IS ONE
LONG PROCESS
OF GETTING
TIRED."

Samuel Butler (1835–1902)

"WHY FEAR DEATH? IT IS THE MOST BEAUTIFUL ADVENTURE IN LIFE."

CHARLES FROHMAN (Broadway producer, 1856–1915), his last words spoken after giving his life-belt to another passenger and then drowning in the sinking of *RMS Lusitania*

"I am ready to meet my MAKER. Whether my MAKER is prepared for the great ordeal of meeting me is another matter."

SIR WINSTON CHURCHILL (1874–1965)

"The hours I spent with thee,
dear heart,
Are as a string of pearls
to me,
I count them over,
every one apart,
My rosary."

ROBERT CAMERON
ROGERS (1862–1912)

"No coward soul is mine,
No trembler in the world's
storm-troubled SPHERE
I see Heaven's glories SHINE,
And faith SHINES equal,
arming me from fear."

EMILY BRONTË (1818–1855),
the last lines she wrote

"GRIEF IS ITSELF A MEDICINE."

William Cowper (1731–1800)

"DRINK TO ME!"

Pablo Picasso (1881–1973)

"*Whenever evil befalls us, we ought to ask ourselves, after the first suffering, how we can turn it into good. So shall we take occasion, from one bitter root, to raise perhaps many flowers.*"

LEIGH HUNT (1784–1859)

"*I am just going* OUTSIDE *and may be some time.*"

Captain Lawrence Edward
Grace Oates
(English explorer, 1880–1912)

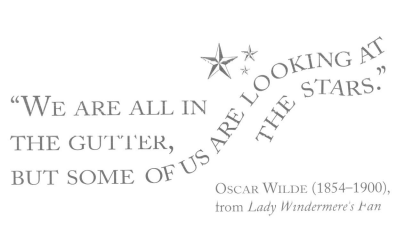

"WE ARE ALL IN THE GUTTER, BUT SOME OF US ARE LOOKING AT THE STARS."

OSCAR WILDE (1854–1900),
from *Lady Windermere's Fan*

"Healing takes COURAGE, *and we all have* COURAGE, *even if we have to dig a little to find it."*

dig.
dig.
dig

TORI AMOS (1963–)

"SO LITTLE DONE, SO MUCH TO DO."

CECIL JOHN RHODES (1853–1902), his last words

Sources &
Acknowledgments

The publishers are grateful for permission to reproduce extracts from works in copyright.

Pages 10 and 33: From *The Dalai Lama's Book of Wisdom* edited by Matthew E. Bunson, published by Rider. Reprinted by permission of The Random House Group Ltd.

Pages 22 and 51: From *Diana* by Sarah Bradford, copyright © 2006 by Sarah Bradford. Used by permission of Viking Penguin, a division of Penguin Group (USA) Inc.

Every effort has been made to contact copyright holders and acknowledge sources, but the publishers would be glad to hear of any omissions.

Index of Authors